StoneSoup

Writing and art by

Editor's Note

Does anything say summer fun and adventure more than this issue's cover art, *Summer Summer*, by Kaavya Killawala? I just want to jump in and be part of it! But as Micki Mermelstein learns in her opening memoir, "Drowning in a Memory," adventure often comes with risk.

This season, we give you a wide spectrum of emotions and themes. It's summer with an introspective twist. There are poems about falling, about swallows in the moonlight, about waves and sun and the spiritual experience of looking at the stars. But summer is also about escape, and we have that too—with the funny story of a hermit crab who stands up to his bullies and not one but two fantasy stories to lose yourself in.

We close with the final installment of *War and Pieces* by Alice Pak. It's been an unflinching look at a friendship divided by war, but I find myself soothed by the note of hope it ends on.

I encourage you to keep writing and creating this summer. Let the time away from school clear your mind so you can explore new ideas and new ways of expressing yourself. There's no time like the summer to take a creative risk!

Happy adventuring!

D Landeff

Thank You to Our Donors!

Production and publication of this issue is made possible by our Jane Austen donors ($1,000 and above):

The Allen & Eve Foundation, Sandy & Tom Allen, Anonymous (4), James Evarts, Amanda Fox, Brian Harlan, Gerry Mandel, Brion Sprinsock & Kristine Albrecht, Sally & Clem Wood.

Cover:
Summer Summer (Oil pastel crayons)
Kaavya Killawala, 11
India

Diane Landolf

Production Coordinator
Kelly Holler

Typesetter
Naomi Kinsman

Communications
Tayleigh Greene

Blog Editor
Olivia McKeon

Refugee Project
Laura Moran

Director Emeritus
William Rubel

Stone Soup (ISSN 0094 579X) is published bimonthly, six times per year. Copyright © 2024 by the Children's Art Foundation–Stone Soup Inc., a 501(c)(3) nonprofit organization located in Santa Cruz, California. All rights reserved.

Thirty-five percent of our subscription price is tax-deductible. Consider further supporting *Stone Soup*—visit stonesoup.com/donate.

To request the braille edition of *Stone Soup* from the National Library of Congress, call +1 800-424-8567. To request access to the audio edition via the National Federation of the Blind's NFB-NEWSLINE®, call +1 866-504-7300, or visit Nfbnewsline.org.

StoneSoup Contents

STORIES

11 Laiomi and the Dragons
Felicia Johnson

18 The Forest
Callia Rodgers

28 Rise Up
Autumn E. Weinreich

53 War and Pieces (Part III)
Alice Pak

MEMOIR

5 Drowning in a Memory
Micki Mermelstein

36 Rats!
Siddharth Mukherjee

43 A New Home
Mark Chen

POETRY

7 state of peace
Sylvie Zubaty

8 Two Poems
Lillian Power

15 Swallows
Ida Wiesenfeld

16 Lime Tree
Gia Koo

33 Little Bay Soup
Marilena Korahais

35 Gone Feeding
Petros Korahais

38 Questions
Marielle Miller

40 A lot of nature with a little bit of red
Ethan Issadore

42 If You Find a Mirror
Sophia Famolari

47 Two Poems
Sierra Elman

51 Untitled
Nadia Darity

ART

Cover:
Summer Summer
Kaavya Killawala

4 Lonely Little Cottage
Ishika Chakrobartty

10 Ode to the Sea
Siddharth Mukherjee

17 Lush giant tree
Eashua Yu-Xue Su

27 Rock, of The Arrvynn Adventures
Xanthe Trim

32 Ramen
Carina Li

39 Spacing Out
Leticia Cheng

41 Crayons
Liana Aeder

46 Fractals
Anushka Trivedi

48 Flaming Blankets
Roi Aeder

50 The Flowerpot
Stuti Jain

52 Fall 1
Jason Jun

62 Highlight from Stonesoup.com

63 Honor Roll

Lonely Little Cottage (Prisma colored pencils)
Ishika Chakrobartty, 10
Texas

Drowning in a Memory

Micki faces her fears by jumping off a cliff

By Micki Mermelstein, 12
Los Angeles, California

I had always had a fear of heights. However, it was pretty inconsequential and did not play a significant role in my life. I was forced to overcome it if I wanted to tag along with my older cousins and keep up with the next activity or adventure they were planning. This time, it was to off to Blueberry Island. The island was an uninhabited rocky outcropping near my grandparents' lake house in Montreal, Canada, accessed by kayak or motorboat. It was known for its abundant growth of wild blueberries every summer, hence its nickname.

Jumping off a cliff is never my idea of fun, even if I have done it before. Or so I was made to believe. Since my cousins had pressured me into doing all sorts of crazy things with them in the past, I took it at face value when I was told that this was no big deal and that of course I had jumped from the highest point off Blueberry Island before. As it turned out, my cousins were wrong.

"Ready?" my cousin Sam asked me.

"Sure, but you're going first," I replied, squinting in the sunlight that was dancing on the water below me, the towering evergreens swaying slightly on the distant shore.

"Okay."

"Three, two, one!" I counted down for him as he ran straight off the cliff, plummeting into the shimmering depths, about thirty-five feet below.

Then it was my turn. I took a few deep breaths and then hurled myself off the cliff, following his lead. I thought I would glide elegantly through the air, smoothly slicing into the water. But it was the complete opposite. My descent was more like an unrestrained freefall and less like a graceful swan dive. Straight down, like a dead weight, with wind rushing through my ears, seemingly endless. And yet, despite my freefall, it seemed as though I actually had time. I was aware of my body moving, my arms flailing as I tried to stay balanced. It was like my universe was in slo-mo even though it was simultaneously on time-lapse.

As soon as I hit the surface, I was in shock. Total stupor, my body numb. Pushing through the coldness of the water. I knew I must be okay, right? After all, over the years every single one of my cousins had done this jump many times before, and each and every one of them had survived.

A few seconds later, all of that changed. The coldness seeped in, saturating my lungs. I couldn't breathe; I was gasping for air. I tried propelling my arms through the water, but I couldn't tell which way was up, or which way was down. I couldn't see, the water burning my eyes. I squeezed them shut, though that proved to be an even bigger mistake. My life flashed before my eyes. The memories from that school year, times with my family, my cousins urging me to attempt the inconceivable. All of a sudden, I had a thought. A singular thought, in this moment of panic. That I would never surface. That I would never get to spend another summer at the lake house. Never have the opportunity to say a final goodbye to my friends. Not even a parting hug to my parents back home or a closing farewell to my cousins.

No sooner than that thought blanketed my mind in a heavy veil, I repelled it back. I still had a chance. A chance to escape. A chance to live. With one powerful kick, I thrust myself to the surface, gasping for breath, the sun's rays painting my face. I painstakingly swam to the boat, still dazed, choking and coughing, purging every droplet of the brackish lake water I had swallowed. I rested my head on the ledge of the motorboat's swim platform, depleted, catching my breath.

After a few seconds, my chest still heaving, my grandfather called out to me.

"Micki," he said, "do it again. You were too quick. I didn't get a chance to video your jump for your mom."

I couldn't tell whether or not he was joking, but somehow my head, still enshrouded in fog, bobbed up and down. Yes, I would do it all again. I swam back to shore, scrambled up the cliff, and ran, never looking back.

state of peace

By Sylvie Zubaty, 12
California

have you ever wondered what it feels like to fly?
flying is falling, just in a different direction.
jumping is swimming, just from a different angle.
sometimes I wonder what weightlessness feels like.
i walk towards the edge of the
cliff.
i wish I was a bird.
birds are like rockets.
rockets are like life.
you grow, and grow, and grow, until you return to your original state of
nothingness
i forget what nothingness feels like.
nothingness must be like weightlessness,
just like falling is like flying.
but if falling is weightlessness, is flying nothingness?
weightlessness is tranquility, in its most pronounced form.
i long for tranquility.
the purely tranquil state seems like a dream
dreams are like salad;
they make you feel healthy, and joyous until
you choke on the random peppercorn that just had to be there.
if falling is weightlessness, and weightlessness is tranquility, then i wish to
fall.
to be at peace.
i turn around and face the mountain.
i grip the jagged rocks and climb
up, up, higher and higher,
until I am taller than the stars.
i reach up, and i grasp the sun in the palm of my hand.
i have reached the top of the world.
and now i shall
fall

Two Poems

By Lillian Power, 11
Texas

Beautiful

As I came out of my skin
I had no idea
How beautiful I was when I bloomed
I was white, yellow, blue, and green
Me

And as I thought to myself
The sky is blue
The grass is green
Dotted with pictures
My past, my present
This is how it was meant to be
I am Me

Free Waters

I wish the world could see me now
The waves are light
The winds are soft
I left my army up on land
Defenseless, I stand

Whispers inside my head
What I never thought would ever end
I close my eyes, I listen

My costume gone, I leave the earth
I set my coat on a hook
The whispers never hold me now
A clear voice has found me somehow
I listen, I follow

I never want to see tomorrow
When whispers will come back again
And my feet will rest upon the land
They say that it is safer there
But I am not scared of the waters

True
Defenseless
Silent
Waters
Free Waters

Ode to the Sea (Acrylic and pastel)
Siddharth Mukherjee, 12
California

Laiomi and the Dragons

An elf girl tries to stop a dragon attack on her kingdom

By Felicia Johnson, 10
Minnesota

"What should we do about these attacks?" the knight said to his co-worker. "I don't know . . . They've only happened in the outskirts of the kingdom so far. Not a lot of people have been hurt yet . . ."

The other knight responded: "Nevertheless, those dragons have to be stopped."

Laiomi, who had been so entranced in the conversation that she had leaned out from her hiding spot behind one of the palace gates, quickly snapped back to behind the gate so she wouldn't be seen.

The knights wouldn't want a fifteen-year-old elf girl listening in on their conversation.

The sun was starting to set, and Laiomi figured she should get home (although she would have liked to snoop on the knights some more).

Sighing, she started down the cobblestone path leading away from the palace.

"Dragons . . . dragons . . . I wonder if they're going to attack Ailiniae," Laiomi muttered to herself.

Ailiniae was the kingdom Laiomi lived in. It was beautiful, with tons of nature, and ornately carved buildings around every corner. But Laiomi didn't live in one of these buildings; she lived in a small cottage with her mother and sister.

As she was walking along the path, immersed in her own thoughts, she heard a loud rustle coming from the forest.

She paused and looked into the thick foliage, hoping to see the creature that had made the noise.

Instead, she saw a large, looming black shadow stretching across the forest floor. Could it be the shadow of . . . a dragon? Laiomi rubbed her eyes. There couldn't possibly be a dragon in the forest.

She saw the warm glow of her cottage and quickly hurried to it. She opened the door, and inside were her mother's and sister's welcoming faces.

"You were gone so late we were getting worried," her mother said. "What in the world were you doing?"

"Spying on the knights," Laiomi said. Laiomi's sister, whose name was Elinor and who was only ten years old, giggled with delight.

"Oooh, what did they say?" she asked.

She felt her feet moving, walking out of the small cottage and into the stillness of the night.

"They said that the dragon attacks are getting worse, and that they might attack the kingdom."

"Oh . . . well . . . maybe the Dragon Charmer will come and save us!" Elinor suggested. Legend had it that if dragons were attacking the kingdom of Ailiniae, a brave young man with the power to charm dragons would come and stop them.

"Maybe, dear," said her mother, although she looked rather worried.

Laiomi sighed. If dragons did attack, their only chance of survival would be the Dragon Charmer coming, however small that chance might be.

Suddenly a sly smile spread across Elinor's face. Laiomi followed her eyes up to the battered clock that hung on the wall. "Why Elinor, you little rascal! It's way past your bedtime!" Laughing, her mother said, "Go to bed, Elinor! You need to get enough sleep." Elinor giggled and jumped onto her small bed.

A few hours later, both Laiomi's sister and mother were fast asleep. Laiomi gazed out of the open window, from which a cool breeze was making its way into the house.

Laiomi closed her eyes, enjoying the quiet sensation. But this only lasted for a few seconds; a ferocious roar split through the air.

Laiomi's family didn't wake up, for they were still very deep in sleep. But the roar still rang through her ears, and it felt as though some invisible force was trying to get her to find the noise's creator.

She felt her feet moving, walking out of the small cottage and into the stillness of the night. Her thoughts became rather muddled and dazed. Although she didn't know where this invisible force was taking her, she knew that she had some sort of job to do there.

That thought pounded in her brain just as her heart pounded in her chest. She had a responsibility. The invisible force had told her that much. She just didn't know what it was yet . . .

Her feet had carried her to the edge of the forest. A sharp pain split through her head, and suddenly her thoughts returned to normal. She let out a small gasp, for she had had no idea what had just happened. Then, out from the dense trees and thickets of bushes came a dragon.

It had shimmering red scales, large orange eyes, and a pair of glittering wings. It was around two times as tall as Laiomi.

She stumbled backward. Her brain was telling her to run, move, do something, but every inch of her was frozen to the spot.

Then, her pair of hazel eyes met the dragon's orange ones, and something amazing happened.

It happened slowly. She could feel her soul melding with the dragon's, as easily as a blacksmith melded gold with silver.

And suddenly, she understood. She understood the attacks, and the dragons, and all of it. And she knew that she could help. The dragon had summoned her there. And it had told her something.

"All this time," Laiomi whispered to the dragon. "All this time, it hasn't been you attacking. It's been us."

The so-called dragon attacks hadn't been the dragons attacking the people at all. It had been the people attacking the dragons. Visions of dragons lying injured on the ground flashed through her head. Her stomach twisted with anger and revulsion.

"Please tell me," Laiomi said to the dragon. "How can I help?"

Minutes later, Laiomi was walking toward the palace, determined and focused.

The dragon flew silently beside her. They got to the palace door, which was flanked by two guards. When the guards saw the dragon, they immediately raised their spears and began to bellow "Dragon!" so that other knights would come to their aid.

Laiomi muttered "Oh, just stop" and pushed past them.

The dragon, who was too big to fit through the door, flew up above the palace so no one could catch it.

The guards and knights probably would have chased after Laiomi, but they were far too preoccupied with the dragon, who was now circling above the West Tower.

Laiomi walked down the polished marble halls until she came to the large throne room doors. She pushed them open, and on the red velvet throne sat the king.

"Do you wish to speak with me?" asked the king.

"Yes, Your Majesty," answered Laiomi. "You see, I think I have a way to stop the attacks."

So she told him what she knew; about how the people had been attacking the dragons and this was why the dragons had been hurting the people.

"And how have you gotten this information?" asked the king.

"Well . . . I saw a dragon in the forest last night. In fact, it might kind of . . . be flying around the palace right now. . . . Anyway! Our eyes met, and it just . . . told me. I think that most problems in the world could be solved if we just listened to each other," she finished.

The king nodded. "Interesting . . . but supposedly the only person who can understand dragons is the Dragon Charmer."

Laiomi was puzzled. According to legend, the Dragon Charmer would be a man.

Suddenly, the queen swept into the room, her long skirts billowing after her.

"I overheard your conversation," she said, "and I want you to know, girl, that you don't have to be a man to do amazing things. I believe that you're the Dragon Charmer. In fact, I just saw the dragon that you were talking about."

"Well then," said the king. "If my wife believes it, so do I. I'll send my knights to stop those attackers. But only if you promise to keep those dragons from attacking any people. Do we have a deal?"

"Yes, Your Majesty."

It was late morning when Laiomi walked home from the palace, the dragon flying beside her.

She hoped that her mother and sister weren't too worried about her. She couldn't wait to tell them everything that had happened.

She smiled; she thought that everything would be peaceful from here.

Swallows

By Ida Wiesenfeld, 13
United Kingdom

At the crack of dawn,
In the cloudless sky,
Gulps of swallows perched on silver firs,
Sing blithely to the wakening sun.

When the sun bleeds its velvet wounds,
Tainting the sky in crimson hues,
Flocks of darkly plumaged swallows,
Graze the sunlit waters, fringing it with shadows.

When the sky is shrouded by an ebony cloak of stars,
And the moon hangs at a perfect crescent,
The swallows come aloft,
Silent and obscured by the unfurling twilight.

Their wingtips brush past the moon,
Their wings no longer black, are now tasseled with moonlight.

Lime Tree

By Gia Koo, 6
United Kingdom

Lovely lime leaf tree marching in the gloomy woods.
In winter leaves sadly die. Birds chirp a beautiful song.
My goodness, look how much you've grown! I said one sunny day.
Every year lime leaves overflow the autumnal woods.

Lush giant tree (Poster paints and aluminum foil)
Eashua Yu-Xue Su, 11
Taiwan

The Forest

After the loss of her mother, Elara discovers her true birthright

By Callia Rodgers, 13
British Columbia, Canada

It was all a blur. The tears, the confusion, the stupid sympathetic but awkward "What do I do now?" looks on the doctors' faces as they watched my face drop, and the tears start spilling out. I couldn't even cry anymore; the truth had burrowed into my brain and now just sat there. No emotions, no thoughts, just "Oh. I guess that happened." How was I supposed to sleep now? I stared at the ceiling. I was awake. Not from sadness, but from utter boredom. I covered my head with my pillow as the baby started another crying fit. Her cries echoed through my head. Haunting me. The new baby was the whole reason this had happened, and yet now she was in bed with my dad, crying about some dumb thing like being hungry, or being tired or needing a diaper change. She didn't understand the pain, and probably never would.

The baby cried for the millionth time since she was born. Which was yesterday. I needed a break.

"Dad, I'm going outside," I said drowsily, putting my shoes on. He rushed out to stop me.

"Wait. You need to read this first. I already did. It's from your mother," he mumbled. I almost couldn't tell his wife had died yesterday. Almost. He still stuttered over the word "mother," and looked at the ground as he said it. Making the words barely audible. I stared at him questioningly and pulled the letter out of the envelope. Seeing the curvy handwriting of my mother almost made me break down in tears. This was probably the last letter my mother had ever written. Somehow, I held in the tears, saving them in my mental bucket. When it overflowed, there would be no way to stop the sobs and they would cascade down my face in waterfalls for hours. I read the letter:

Dear Elara (and Nick),

I really don't want to have to do this, but after I die, you can no longer go into the forest. I'm so sorry, love. I know the forest means everything to you, and I don't want to have to take it away from you, but it is simply too dangerous and unpredictable now that I'm gone. Please forgive me.
—Mom

I stared at my dad in disbelief.

"What? No, you can't. I—I have to go there!" I shouted.

My dad looked at the ground and mumbled some more. "Elara, I think it's better if you stay inside right now." After a few awkward seconds, I reluctantly followed him upstairs. Just then the baby started another crying fit, and Dad rushed to shut her up. I sat on the couch and stared blankly at the wall. The forest was the only part I had left of my mother, and now I didn't even have that. I felt like sobbing, ripping my hair out, screaming all over again. I couldn't do this. I didn't know how anyone could. I was alone. So alone. I had nobody to talk to, nobody to play with, nobody to pass the time with. All I could do was sit and stare at the wall watching the time pass as the baby cried again. And again. And again. I was just a blob. I couldn't think, couldn't speak. I could barely walk. The sky was starting to darken. I sighed; I had been staring at the wall for hours. I would never have done that if Mom was still here. Slowly, I stood up and stumbled to bed.

I woke up the next morning. Despite my sadness and hopelessness the night before, I felt confident and happy. But I hid my smile and stumbled sleepily out into the kitchen.

"Good morning, Ela," Dad mumbled, the circles under his eyes telling me exactly how his night went.

"Morning." I smiled, forgetting that I was supposed to be sad. Dad didn't smile back, though the slightest hint of amusement hit his face.

"Someone slept well," he decided. His voice held a slightly painful tinge of bitterness and jealousy.

"Sorry, Dad," I muttered under my breath, and then I waited. I had already put on socks and my favorite sweater over my pajama shirt. As soon as the baby started crying, I went for it. I couldn't help myself from smiling guiltily and mischievously as I slipped my shoes on and begged silently for the door not to creak. *Creaaaaaakkk.* I grimaced but opened the door quickly and slipped outside.

I breathed in the fresh air of the meadow and brushed my hand against the long grass beside me. I watched the forest grow closer as I walked, and my heart beat faster as its tall evergreen trees towered over me. I sighed. This was it. I was about to see my mother again, or at least partially.

"Elara!" a voice called from behind me. I turned, my smile fading when I saw who it was. "Get back inside. Now," my dad yelled. The baby, for once, was not crying. Instead, she lay over my dad's shoulder, drooling on the spit up-covered cloth. I blushed guiltily and followed him inside.

"Elara, this is unacceptable. I can't have you running off whenever I am in the other room looking after your sister." I cringed. "I have no choice but to ground you." I stared at him.

"What?" I said in disbelief. "But—you—why?!" My dad didn't reply; he just went into the kitchen to feed the baby.

"Well no wonder I tried to leave. You've only talked to me twice since it happened; both times it was about the stupid rule that mom made," I muttered. Dad didn't seem to hear me. Instead, he decided to tell me about the third-worst thing I would ever experience in my life. Coincidently, they had all happened in the last week.

"You're going to start school next week," he said. He dropped it on me just like that. No sympathetic "I'm sorry, Elara, but Sedalia is more important than you" or "I can't homeschool you like your mother did because you're a troublemaker, unlike my sweet baby, Sedalia."

I didn't respond. I just walked calmly to my bedroom so that I could explode. I couldn't keep myself calm for one more second. The tears fell; they pooled on my bedroom floor and the carpet sucked them in. I threw my pillow at the wall until I had no energy left to do even that. My dad hadn't even come to see what was wrong.

My grandma came over the next morning. I had only seen her at family dinners on Christmas and Thanksgiving and that was it, but now she was here, ready to pick me up for a girls' shopping day. Hooray. Her face was droopy and wrinkled, but she was healthy for a seventy-year-old. Dad hugged me goodbye, but only after carefully changing Sedalia's diaper, and then Grandma led me out the door to her car. It was a miserable shopping trip. Apparently my Dad had called Grandma and asked her if she would take me out to get some school supplies.
He probably told her it would "take my mind off of things, and get me out of the house."

You know what else would do the same thing but better? If he let me go into the forest instead of being so insistent on enforcing mom's rule. Instead he sent me away with my grandma, who I hadn't seen in over a year, to go shopping for pencils. Probably so that I wouldn't be tempted to run off again. He was too busy with his beloved Sedalia to stop me, so he recruited someone else to do it for him.

"How about this one?" Grandma smiled, holding up a flowery pink pencil case labeled *All-in-one pencil case: with all the school supplies already there!*

I took one look at it and frowned. The contents read: a glue stick, scissors, highlighters, pens, and the pencil case! The "All-in-one *pencil* case" didn't even include a pencil. We ended up leaving the store with nothing. Grandma took me to a few other stores. Eventually we went home without buying anything.

"How did it go?" asked Dad

"It was horr—" I started.

"Great! Elara is so sweet. I would love to see her more often," Grandma

Now, if I screamed and ran away, there was no one to stop me from going too far.

interrupted, glancing at me, smiling. I looked down and rolled my eyes at the floor. When I looked up, my dad was glaring at me. Then he looked away.

"It would be great if you could come tomorrow and again on the weekend," Dad said.

That was my cue to leave. I spent the next while walking around my bedroom grumbling to myself about how unfair it was that I had to go to school. Until now I had been homeschooled. By Mom. She had barely ever given me boring assignments like paper worksheets. When I learned math for the first time, Mom had taken me out into the forest and asked me to count all the trees around me. I had counted twenty before realizing I had missed a lot of trees and lost track halfway through. There, she had taught me how to estimate. We had looked at a group of ten trees and counted how many of those sized groups we could see. We ended up estimating that in the area we covered in our walk, there were about 1,500 trees. The next day we went back and found a little hole with some mice inside; we counted six. Then we set up a picnic and waited. One of the mice left, and without letting me walk up to count the mice that were now left in the hole, she taught me how to subtract. We sat there for a long time watching the mice come and go. By the end, there were eleven mice in the hole. When I learned multiplication, division, algebra, and geometry, she had also taken me into the forest, counting random things. Science was my favorite subject. We would bring out a basket, but instead of it being filled with sandwiches, cheese, and crackers, it was filled with microscopes, acids, and chemicals. We would study beetles under the microscope, their vibrant colors shining in the light. We would dip different types of leaves in the acids. We always had to make sure each and every bug was off of them, because if I saw a single dead bug floating in the bubbly liquid, I would scream and run into the woods, never far enough to get lost, before my mother chased me down and scooped me into her arms, both of us laughing. Now, if I screamed and ran away, there was no one to stop me from going too far. No one to pick me up, a smile covering my face and the silent air carrying our cheerful laughter. Now, all I could do was keep running into the darkness, and if I got too tired to run and scream any longer, I would have to sit in front of a tree and cry until I fell asleep. The darkness would fall over me, and I would never find my way back.

The next morning, I woke up to my dad yelling my name. Eventually, when his endless calls annoyed me enough, I got out of bed.

"What, Dad?" I said, my words slurred and my voice cracked.

"Your grandmother is going to be here in less than five minutes. I'll ask her to get you breakfast, but get ready quickly," he explained.

"Okay," I replied.

Then I started doing the exact opposite. I brushed my teeth for about five minutes, which made them feel nice, but my gums tasted like raw flesh and blood. By then my grandma had already arrived, and my dad was standing with her awkwardly by the door, yelling at me every few seconds to hurry up. I didn't. I brushed my hair extra well, making sure not to rip the pretty, long brown curls. I even tried the lip gloss that had been sitting in my drawer for months. I got dressed slowly, and by the time I was down the stairs, Dad was looking at me angrily and Grandma was cooing to Sedalia, who was staring up at her. I looked at Sedalia. I had probably laid in Grandma's arms just like that many times before, just like I did the same thing with my dad. Now Dad would barely look at me, and he was sending me off with Grandma. Until he had school to send me to instead. Tears started pooling in my eyes. Why did I even have to go to school? Mom had told me she had already taught me most of the things that regular grade tens were learning. The only reason to go to school would be so that Dad could send me somewhere so that he could take care of *cute little Sedalia* and not worry about me running off to the forest every second he went off to care for her.

"Ready to go, Se—I mean, Elara?" asked Grandma.

Typical. Even she cared about Sedalia more than she cared about me. Of course she thought Sedalia was cuter. I said goodbye to my dad without even looking at the baby, and walked out the door.

We arrived home, and Grandma drove up to the curb and I hopped out of the car quickly. She had somewhere to be, so she couldn't come in. I walked slowly to the door, waiting for her to drive away. Once she did, I made a run for it. I ran through the meadow, the grass sweeping my legs and tickling my ankles. The air blew around me, forcing me to close my eyes. I could feel the forest growing closer, the tall trees towering over me and the dark shade blocking out the sunlight and the heat. When I thought I was close enough, I slowed down and opened my eyes. Without another thought, I stepped into the forest.

I walked along the path, the pine needles and gravel somehow completely silent as I stepped over them. I looked around in wonder. The trees were covered in moss. It climbed up them like bumpy green snakes. I didn't feel like screaming when I walked past the spot where Mom and I used to have picnics. I even sat down there and enjoyed the memories of our picnics. I imagined my happiness last time we were here. I could almost hear our laughter still echoing and bouncing from tree to tree. But the last time we were here was almost a year ago. Mom hadn't come here since she got pregnant. She had told me I could take a break from school that year, that I had already learned all the stuff my grade needed to know. As well as the grades ahead, so that year she had spent most of her time either at the doctor, or with my dad talking about baby names, gender-reveal parties,

The trees around me seemed to grow taller, the shadows darker, and the path curvy and long.

baby showers, and all that. When we played board games, if we ever had time to start one, we never had time to finish it. I thought as soon as the baby was born, my life would go back to normal. Obviously, it hadn't. Now I walked through the forest. Despite the chaos, tears, and screams of the past week, I felt normal, like my mom was right there walking by my side, like in her hand swinging forward and backward was our hand-weaved picnic basket, filled with a delicious lunch we had made ourselves, with my favorite picnic blanket tucked into the bottom. Mom had made it before I was born. It had square patches of different fabrics, and I always loved staring at the different pictures. It was almost as if I had gone back in time. If my dad noticed I was gone, he would never find me.

I started running, the wind brushing past my face again and blowing my hair behind me in long flowing strands. I only stopped when I was too tired to take one more step. I sat down beside a tree trying to slow my quick breathing and beating heart, but as darkness fell on the forest, my heavy eyelids fell closed and I fell asleep.

Elara... ELARA!!! I jumped, waking myself up. I wasn't in the forest anymore; I was in a meadow, and there were butterflies flying around my head. The sun sparkled instead of burning through my eyelids or being painfully bright. The grass was replaced by wildflowers, their pollen being taken by all sorts of flying insects and birds.

Elara, wake up and run home. Run home and never come back. They're coming. It was my mom's voice, and it was surprisingly soothing.

"Yes, Mom," I said, dazed. Without realizing what she meant, or who "they" were. The meadow faded to black, and then the forest formed around me. I stood up, and without thinking I started running down the path. I had been running for a long time when I suddenly stopped. I didn't recognize any of the trees around me. I turned around and started running that way, but I didn't recognize anything that way either. I spun in a circle, my heart beating fast. I was lost. The trees around me seemed to grow taller, the shadows darker, and the path curvy and long.

I panicked and ran some more. I didn't know where I was going. I just ran hoping that somehow I would find my way out of the dark woods, and home. At one point I thought I found the clearing where me and Mom used to have picnics, but when I looked around there were twenty more clearings that looked exactly the same. I was lost. I dropped down in the clearing and hugged my knees. The tears spilled out of my eyes again. The trees and shadows blurred and became blobs. One spot got brighter and clearer. I got a weird sensation, like I was a magnet being pulled towards the light. My eyes still blurry from the tears, I walked towards it. The light dimmed when my eyes cleared, but I knew it had to be that way. There was no other way to go.

I walked as quickly as I could that way, but by the time night had fallen again, it felt like I had made no progress at all. I slumped down. Defeated. I would never find my way home. To make matters worse, I felt like I was being watched. A shadow burst through the trees. I turned and watched where I had seen it out of the corner of my eye. Nothing moved. After a few minutes, another shadow seemed to scurry past. But as soon as I turned its way, it disappeared. I turned away. This time it seemed as if two shadows passed on either side of me. When I turned, I saw them. They towered over me. The air around them floated in strands of darkness. I screamed. My heart beating, I stood to run. I ran harder than I ever had before, but they were faster, and there were more of them ahead of me. I wished my beating heart would slow down and stop the blood from rushing through my head so fast. Soon I was surrounded by the monsters. I shielded my eyes and tried to back away, but it was no use. They reached out to touch me. I felt a pang of guilt; my dad would never know what happened to me.

I held up my hand to block them. Light pierced my eyelids. It wasn't orange or yellow like the sun; it was bright blue. When it faded, I opened my eyes. The monsters had backed off a bit, and my hand tingled as if I'd dipped it in some kind of acid. What had I done? A monster came up to me, its fingers grazing my baggy sweater, just before another stream of light came down, making the monster cry out in agony and disappear. I looked up to the source of the light, but the darkness hid whoever was hiding in the shadows. Whoever had just saved my life. I stared up into the shadows, looking for a sign that someone was there, but I couldn't see anything, and the remaining monsters were floating toward me. I ran through a gap in the circle of darkness. As I ran, I heard someone coming after me. Their eyes staring into my back. I ran harder.

"Elara, wait." The voice of my mother flowed through my brain. It hadn't come through my ears; it was as if it had always been there. The voice echoed everywhere in my brain and I stopped. Everything in my body seemed to shut down; I no longer had control of my body. I turned and walked toward the bright blue light behind me.

The form floated smoothly over the gravel- and pine needle-covered path. As it grew closer, I could make out the facial features. The flowing long hair, but instead of blonde it had changed to a light, transparent blue. The nose was long and pointed, the eyes that were usually pretty hazel were now a slightly darker shade of blue, and the wrinkles that never changed how old she looked still sat there, but not as deep.

"Mom?" I said, even though I knew it was her. I had felt her presence ever since I had entered the forest.

"Yes. I think it's time you went home. Your father is worried about you," she said. Her bright blue lips moved, but the sound came from everywhere in the forest. Without a word, I followed her. When we saw a shadow, she pushed her light toward it. Making it creep back into the depth of the forest. But every time she did so, she lost a little color. Her form fading and becoming more transparent.

"Listen. I know this is a lot to take in, but I don't have much time. I'm losing my light," she said after we walked for a while. "Elara. Hold up your hand. Like this." She held up her hand in the direction of a tree. Then when I had copied her, she adjusted my hand, touching my fingers and sending tingling sensations up them. This seemed to make her even more transparent. I worried she would fade away too soon.

"Now. Close your eyes."

I closed my eyes.

"Elara! Quick, it's coming." Before I could open my eyes, bright light shot through my eyelids. I opened my eyes.

"Did you do that?" My hand tingled with new power, and when I looked at my hand, it looked pale and wrong.

"No, Elara. You, like me, are one of the only *Luxrae* left in the world," she started. I interrupted.

"Wait . . . what?!" I demanded. My mother just smiled at me.

"Oh yes. Why do you think I got called down to be the protector of the forest once again? How do you think you shot light out of your hand, and somehow those *Umbrae* disappeared?" She said it in a weird, other world-sounding accent. The kind of accent you would expect some type of fairie to have. Which I guess she is. I guess I am. When I still stared at her, confused, she sighed and started from the beginning.

"Elara, Luxrae are like fairies. We are the protectors of the world. I am a *Luxsil*; I protect the forest. There are other types of Luxrae, like *Luxmar*. We must protect the world from the evil *Noxrae* and Umbrae. Now I must pass my role on to you," she explained.

"Then why didn't you want me to go into the forest?" I wondered.

"Because I was worried; my sister and I were full Luxrae. You are only half; I was worried it would be too much for you. I should've taught you; I just ran out of time."

"Wait, you have a sister?" I demanded. I was never told much about my mom's side of the family. I had never even heard about my grandparents, or apparently my aunt.

"Yes. She was my best friend. That's why I decided to give you a sister. Even though I knew Luxrae can only have two children. I thought you would love her. But apparently I was wrong." She smiled sadly

"Wait, what do you mean Luxrae can only have two children. You mean you knew you would die? And you never warned me?" I felt offended, but also guilty. I had spent the first week of my sister's life wishing she didn't exist, when my mom had given up her life for her. Maybe having a sister wasn't so bad. I had a sudden urge to run home; I hadn't ever held a baby before. I hadn't wanted to before, but now suddenly that was the only thing I wanted to do. I started running. Behind me my mother sent me the last of her light, and faded away.

The monsters I ran past crept back. I didn't mind that I hadn't properly said goodbye to my mother; she would always be here. All I had to do was come back.

When I walked through the door and wasted no time asking my dad if I could try holding my sister, he didn't ask questions. He smiled, relieved yet knowingly, and handed Sedalia to me carefully, showing me how to hold her. I stared down at her tiny face, her eyes closed peacefully. Though I can't say I was very pleased when she opened her eyes and spat up all over my face. It kind of ruined the moment. As my dad wiped the spit-up off my face, I rocked her back and forth. She was my favorite baby sister in the whole world. Though there weren't many other options to choose from.

Rock, of The Arrvynn Adventures (Colored pencil)
By Xanthe Trim, 12
United Kingdom

Rise Up

A meek hermit crab is fed up with the bully crabs at school

By Autumn E. Weinreich, 9
Illinois

I wake up to the mechanical beeping of my alarm clock. I sit up rubbing my eye stalks. I climb out of bed and take off my scratchy abdomen cover.

I quickly put on a moss-cotton and coconut fiber one, and then I put on a white shirt with a tree on it, and the four-legged jeans I always wear on my visible legs, and I shove on my blue socks with lobsters on them. Then I scuttle into my comfortable green shell with Norfolk Island stickers all over it.

I grab the lump of wax sitting on my dresser and lump it onto my deep purple claw.

Next, I try to straighten my crimped antennae, but to no avail.

I walk, or rather *krt*, over to my mirror and put on my blue glasses.

Then I shove my visible legs into my recently knitted slippers (they're really cozy), and I walk out of the door of my bedroom. I tiptoe out across the hallway to my little brother's bedroom.

Perfect. The mealworm brain is asleep. I *krt* downstairs to the kitchen.

I open the cupboard to get some freeze-dried mealworms and pour some into a bowl. I quickly gobble them up and then retreat into my shell. I'm usually not allowed to play video games on weekdays, but my friend Kerm gave me her Game Crab over winter break.

I'm on the fifth world of my favorite game, *Explorer Sandbar*, when my mom says, "Kermie, can you wake your brother up?"

Saying that as a question is her basically saying, "Kermit, wake your brother up right now."

I look back to the screen of the Game Crab only to find that it says "Game Over." I sigh and put it back in my jeans, and I walk up the stairs to my brother Jerry's room.

Now, from Jerry's secret stash, I grab the ingredients to wake him up. One can of spinach juice, one tin of calcium powder, one washcloth drenched in saltwater, and three mealworms. Then I take Jerry out of his bed and push him into his shell. He's already a little awake, and before he has time to react, I open the tin of calcium powder and sprinkle some into his face. Then I carefully drizzle ice-cold spinach juice, causing him to wake up suddenly.

I feel as powerless as I would have been in the cold without my shell.

His claws start flailing everywhere, and one slices the bridge of my glasses. I hand him the salt water-covered rag to clean himself up, and I quickly grab some Krabos tape and wrap it around my broken bridge. I throw him the three mealworms.

"Breakfast!" I shout.

I quickly throw him a blue polo shirt and khaki pants. While he's getting dressed, I lump some wax onto his claws. Then I hurry downstairs.

I check the clock. Fifteen minutes! For once, I'm early for school. I quickly pack our bags and pull on my blue coat, gray hat, and black mittens. As soon as Jerry's down, I hand him his coat. Our mom firmly places thermoses of warm fresh water with calcium powder mixed in it on our claws. I quickly run outside, pulling Jerry.

I run into the alley, and I leave Jerry behind as soon as he starts playing with ice as usual.

It is snowing outside, and most hermit crabs would be shivering, but us purple pinchers are a lot hardier than those tropical softies. As soon as I get to school (I'm one of the first crabs there), I hear some all-too-familiar voices.

I quickly bury my nose into *Mosses of the Midwest* and read. Suddenly, a deep voice says, "What do we have here?"

I grimace. Slowly looking up, it's the Stonestock twins and their posse. "I'm reading this wonderful book," I say.

Suddenly, before I can stop myself, my voice gets high-pitched and fast. "It's about mosses. They're nonvascular spore-bearing plants. They're not pteridophytes! Those are vascular spore-bearing plants." My voice trails off.

Theo, the meaner of the twins, snatches it and throws it in a snowdrift.

"But—" I begin.

"What, Four Eyes?!" Theo yells when I don't answer.

He opens my backpack and spills out the contents. I start to need to pee really badly (I do that when I'm nervous) because the first thing he sees is my best knitting needles. "The dweeb knits?" he asks, holding them up, and to my dismay, he starts to break them.

He then drops them into the snow along with my newest knitting project, a hammock. He laughs. Then he snips my broken glasses' tape. I feel as powerless as I would have been in the cold without my shell.

My friends arrive, and soon Lucy's computer and sketchbook, Kerm's eraser collection and giant calculator, and Stanley's craft knives and history book set join my stuff in the snowdrift. Kerm has some tape to fix my glasses, and Lucy can get her computer back, but we're pretty much powerless. Then the bell rings.

I sit through the morning subjects until recess. I hurry to the place where my friends meet outside, behind a few dozen boulders. I'm late, and my friends seem to be discussing what we should do about the mean crabs.

"We should hack into their computers!" exclaims Lucy.

"No, carefully planned battle would be better," puts in Kerm.

"Full-blown war would actually be way more effective," argues Stanley.

"What about you, Kermie?" asks Kerm.

"Oh, I don't know," I say, shifting my legs uncomfortably.

But inside I do. And maybe Kerm won't have to be the crab with the plan. I will.

Soon everybody is arguing. The bell rings for lunch, and tempers have flared, except mine of course. Lunch is OK, but my mealworm sandwich is soggy, and everybody is still arguing. The rest of the day comes and goes quickly, with the exception of gym class. Finally, the school day is done, and me and Stanley walk out the door together.

"Bye, Stan!" I yell at Stanley.

"Bye!" he yells back.

I meet Jerry by the bike racks. "Tell Mommy and Daddy that I'm playing at school," I say, gently pushing him toward the sidewalk.

He nods. I walk toward the athletics field and sit at the old rickety second playground. As usual, Theo and his gang are playing exoball. Usually, I'm here to draw the native plant life, but today this crab has a plan.

I sit up, slowly walking towards Theo.

"What do you want, weirdo?!" he exclaims.

"I—I want payback," I stammer.

"All right. Exoball. Four on four, in four days." He smirks.

"See ya after school!" he yells as I walk away.

"Yeah, see you later, weird-a-gator," Ollie, one of his posse members, shouts.

"After a while, Jock-a-dile!" I shoot back. I can't believe I said that.

"Oh, you are going to pay, nerd turd!" yells Peter, another one of his goons.

I go home only to find that I have to babysit Jerry and his friend Eddie. My pedagogy is to lock them in the playroom with animal crackers and juice boxes, and they will mostly be fine.

Then I work on my exoball outfit. Eddie has to go home now. Phew. And of course we have to have swim lessons and, later, piano. The next few days are a blur, training and school until the big day (and, of course, convincing my friends that we can win the exoball game).

Crowds of siblings and friends have gathered on the bleachers. The game suddenly starts. I wasn't paying attention before, and the last thing I see before I face-plant is a banner that says "Go, Indiana Vader." A weird name, but that's our team's name, and I also see the kid who has managed to get control of the scoreboard. I get back up and someone throws me the ball. The force of it makes me tumble backward. Even though I know the sports shell will bounce, I close my eyes. Strangely enough, I find myself to be floating. I open my eyes and look at the face of Theo. He snatches the ball and throws me to the ground. There is no referee, so he never gets in trouble. He throws the exoball across the field to Peter, which somehow makes them score a bunch of points. Peter never lets go of the ball, and he trips. Lucy falls on top of him and suddenly everybody except me and Theo is in that pile. Theo starts chasing me, and I jump in. After what seems like hours, I somehow emerge with the ball. Theo, who is a few yards away, runs at me. All the training suddenly flows back to me in an instant; I flip over his head, onto his green sports shell.

He turns around in surprise. My friends catch on to what I'm doing, and in an instant they're pretending not to want to get steamrolled by Theo. Both Kerm and Lucy point to Stanley, who pretends he has the ball and runs away from Theo. He pursues him and forgets all about having me on his shell. I bounce off into the point zone, and Indiana Vader takes the lead. I realize I could do this with other crabs on their team. They're all faster than me. The game goes by quickly until I have the ball. I harness the power of Rick, the nicer of the twins, and then Ollie, who switches directions.

Apparently, I was going the wrong way. How could I tell what side is ours and what side is theirs? And then he trips over Rick, who fell down when I jumped. Ollie was already running fast, and I chose the right time to jump, right when he tripped, so I doubled the momentum. Then I landed in the point zone. Right then the buzzer went off, and even though I didn't have my glasses on, I could tell I won the game.

One week later

So many things have changed in just one week. Me and my friends have climbed up two rungs of the social ladder. We have become somebodies.

You probably would never see me enjoy school. But here I am.

We are not just hermit crabs that hide behind boulders. We're crabs that people talk to. Everyone except Theo and his gang is happy about the whole exoball thing. And for me? I'm perfectly content being popular. Personally, I think that if it weren't for me, we never would have won the game.

But I never before imagined life at school turning out like this. This is pure bliss, and I'm happier than anybody's ever been at school. This crab loves it.

Ramen (Colored pencil)
Carina Li, 13
New York

Little Bay Soup

By Marilena Korahais, 13
New York

Start with a bucket of water
Taken straight from the bay
Taste, to ensure it is salty
Look, to ensure it is gray

Find the Little Bay Sand Witch
Borrow a cup of her sand
Ask for the kind that is sweaty
Or I warn you your soup will be bland

Hunt for the shell of a moon snail
Moon snails are found at low tide
Stick your hand deep in the gravel
Deep—to avoid you—they hide

Find the four spikes of an urchin
Cover in jellyfish spread
Garnish with cordgrass and glasswort
And algae, stringy and red

Locate some rocks that are shiny,
For texture, grind up a clam
A spoonful of slimiest seaweed
And the bumps of the bumpiest crab

Now listen, ever so closely
It's called the London tree plane
Gather the bark it has shedded
And add to it a liter of rain

Now stir it all into a whirlpool
And wait for some lightning to strike it
During the full moon of August
It's worth it! I promise you'll like it!

Gone Feeding

By Petros Korahais, 10
New York

"Gone fishing" is misleading,
A phrase some people say
For me, the fish just eat my bait
And then they swim away

Rats!

Siddharth discovers a surprising solution to his family's rat problem

By Siddharth Mukherjee, 12
California

The damp, musty smell filled my nostrils as I carefully switched on the light. Armed with a wooden bat, I warily surveyed the inside of the garage. Cardboard boxes lay scattered everywhere, filled to the brim with a various assortment of items. I put a shaking foot forward, steadying it on the cold, uneven ground.

The light flickered, and I swung the bat to my right. A loud thud echoed through the spooky garage, and I looked at what my bat had hit. It was a cardboard box from Home Depot, with a large tangle of lights and decorations inside it. The word "Christmas" was scrawled across it in big, messy letters. I quickly grabbed the box and ran back into the house.

Last year, my house had a rat problem. Rats had invaded and taken over parts of our house. I remember we had to meow like a cat before entering the garage. The cost of getting rid of the rats and plugging all the holes was much more than $1,000. My mother thought that the cost was too much, so we decided to let nature take its course. At first, we set up some rat traps, but it didn't catch the creature. Instead, I got stuck in one of them while getting our Christmas tree out of the attic, but that's a whole other story.

Our next attempt was letting me concoct a deadly potion and leaving it out for the rat to drink. I took a few drops of thioacetone and mixed it into a glass of milk. I stirred ferociously, trying to dissolve every molecule of the poison into the milk. Thioacetone is a chemical that smells extremely bad and is deadly. The scent of fresh milk overpowered the smell, so the rat wouldn't even notice the smell.

The next morning, the glass into which I poured milk was completely empty. This made us assume that the rat had died, but we discovered fresh traces of rat poop the next day. That meant that the rat and its family had not died, despite the consumption of a deadly chemical.

My next attempt to kill the furry creature was to leave food out on the dining table and then hide underneath it. In theory, when the rat came to nibble away at the food, I would hit it with a twenty-pound weight and squish it. I stayed up the entire night watching TV on my laptop, but no rat came. I went to sleep at around eight a.m., and the entire bowl of food had been devoured by the time I woke up an hour later. I thought rats were nocturnal creatures, but it turned out this one was diurnal.

Finally, one night, my mother left some of her khichuri outside. This was completely accidental, because she had gone up to do something and had forgotten about covering the food. Khichuri is supposed to be an Indian comfort food made with rice and lentils. The way my mom made it, though, was by mixing loads of spices with Quaker Oats porridge.

My dad and my brother made fun of her food, and I did too occasionally because it smelled bad and looked pale green, which was not the color it was supposed to look. It tasted like an apple; some parts were crunchy, while others were flavorless. The next day, we found the rat lying next to the bowl of khichuri.

When my dad (who's a doctor) pressed his ear against the rat and listened for a heartbeat, he shook his head and said, "He's dead." Finally, the rat had died, but only because of my mother's bad cooking.

Questions

By Marielle Miller, 12
Pennsylvania

I wonder what it would be like
To live in a world
Where I sound strange.
I wonder what came after before
But before history.
I'm supposed to wonder,
What? Where? When?
Those are the questions
I'm supposed to ask.
But instead, I always ask,
Why?
I think it's annoying.
I think I don't care.

Spacing Out (Watercolor)
Leticia Cheng, 11
California

A lot of nature with a little bit of red

By Ethan Issadore, 11
Maryland

A lot of nature with a little bit of red,
And that is to be said.
Trees and forests for miles on end.
I forget the cityscape, but I try to pretend.
The branches start to bend,
And then there is a crack.
The fire starts to sizzle and glow, like preparing an attack.
We huddle around the fire,
Though we have one more desire.
At least we do not need to "brrr."
We collect the ingredients and start to stir.
The fire grows higher and higher
In fact, so high
It lights up the night sky.
Our brains start to tire.
Now I can only see darkness and the fire.
We pour the soup into bowls, though it starts to droop.
I go to sleep, though wondering if I'm in a loop.
Am I inevitably waiting for my doom?
Or perhaps I'm trapped inside a room.
But as the night sky fades from night,
I start to see daylight.
Waking up again to see the same sight.
For I am still here, and the wood is still bark.
The sky has turned bluish though still very dark.
I light another match,
I sit down and start to attach.
To reflect how I got here and everything I've said.
As I look at my surroundings,
A lot of nature with a little bit of red.

Crayons (iPhone 15 Pro)
Liana Aeder, 9
New York

If You Find a Mirror

By Sophia Famolari, 11
South Carolina

Look inside
yourself
take your vision of
the world
and turn it
upside down

break the glass
to find your truth

then stitch it up again

consider
every secret
that might be
hidden in its depths
until you
realize
it's only a
reflection
of what you already
know

it only holds
fragments
of what it's like
out here

A New Home

Mark says goodbye to his familiar old apartment and neighborhood

By Mark Chen, 12
New York

I woke with a start to the sight of empty, cavernous blue walls that had just yesterday held my bookshelves, now barren. Pale dawn light seeped in through the curtainless windows. The rhythmic scraping of furniture across worn chestnut floors made me flinch. Downstairs, the symphony of packing tape screeching and boxes being sealed had already begun. I slowly rose from the creaky twin bed that had seen me through countless sleepless nights and milestones, a faithful companion for the past ten years of my life. Soon it would be destroyed, tossed onto an overflowing landfill, forgotten. I ran my fingers over the nicks and scratches on the headboard one last time, saying goodbye. Along with it, I was leaving my room, my apartment that harbored memories of my earliest days—tracing crayon masterpieces on the doors as a toddler, taking my first steps across the scuffed hardwood floors. I was leaving my school, my friends, my life all behind.

I gazed out the balcony window, watching as the inky canvas of night sky transformed into a vibrant watercolor painting of pinks, oranges and yellows. Wispy clouds drifted lazily overhead, illuminated with fiery brilliance as if edged in molten gold by the awakening sun. Below, Yellowstone Playground sprawled, a treasured place I had visited every day for nearly a decade of my childhood. As dawn's glow washed over the playground, memories flooded back. The monkey bars, their rungs worn smooth by my sweaty palms during endless summer afternoons spent honing my skills, now sat empty and silent. The sandbox, holding faint shadows of the elaborate castles and fairytale cities I built only to vanish overnight, appeared untouched by human hands. The swing sets creaked ever so slightly, their rusted chains swaying in the morning breeze after years of use. The basketball courts with their faded paint lines lay dormant, devoid of the perpetual dribbling of balls.

The rising sun's rays stretched across Yellowstone, illuminating the landmarks of my childhood adventures like a bittersweet spotlight. The chains on the swing set glimmered as the light struck the rusted metal links. The sandbox seemed to glow like a treasure chest full of memories buried just beneath the surface. Even the cracked asphalt of the basketball court appeared less worn, momentarily

Even the cracked asphalt of the basketball court appeared less worn, momentarily renewed by the dawn.

renewed by the dawn. As the City That Never Sleeps began to fall silent, I said one final silent goodbye to the playground where skinned knees and first crushes lived alongside hide-and-seek victories and friendships forged. This chapter of my life in this place had come to a close, but the memories would always be a part of me.

Just then, the rumbling of a truck engine shattered the quiet reverie of the morning. I gazed down to see an oversized moving truck turn the corner, its worn tires crunching on the broken concrete outside our building. Stamped on the truck's side I could barely make out the words I knew were hidden beneath the dusty grime of long highways: BELLA'S MOVERS said a faded print on the side. The worn truck pulled to a stop, signaling it was here for its solemn duty— to transport those few precious boxes that contained my childhood within their fragile walls of bubble wrap and styrofoam. As the movers loaded the back of the truck, I felt a swell of memories and a lump form in my throat. My posters, books, toys—my whole world was being taken away in that truck. I realized my years of childhood innocence playing in this playground were well and truly over, about to vanish into the rearview mirror. The truck's engine revved, ready to drive my memories away to whatever unknowns lay ahead next in my life's journey. I took one last long look at my beloved playground, knowing that while my memories could leave this place, they would always dwell deep within my heart.

The echo of my footsteps reverberated off the bare walls and hardwood floors as I did one final walkthrough of my new apartment. Everything was so clean: sharp edges and blank canvas. Moving turned out to be one of the biggest obstacles I've faced in my young life thus far. Leaving the comfort and familiarity of my childhood home felt like being ripped from a warm, soft cocoon and plunged into an odyssey of discovery tinged with loneliness and longing. I would be leaving behind my circle of beloved childhood friends, the faded floral wallpaper in my bedroom that I had memorized over years of lying in bed, the creaky wooden steps leading downstairs that knew my footsteps by heart, the worn but comfortable furnishings that had loyally served me since before I could remember. I would miss our cozy kitchen, scene of so many batches of homemade cookies and late-night snacks, and our living room where we sat together and watched movies. My mother assured me my well-loved toys and stuffed animals would have a new life with my young cousin, and that having a new, bigger home was something to feel proud of. However, as I hesitantly entered our new home for the very first time, the soaring ceilings and cavernous rooms felt cold and sterile. I felt small, insignificant, and out of place amidst the grand, gilded furnishings and lavish new lifestyle I was being introduced to. Though this towering new dwelling was now technically my home, at first I just felt deeply homesick within its unfamiliar walls, longing for the warm familiarity of my childhood abode.

The barren rooms echoed hollowly with each footfall, devoid of any semblance of hominess or personality. This dwelling was but an empty vessel, a blank canvas awaiting my touch. I embarked upon the process of imprinting my essence, commencing with adorning the stark white walls with memories encapsulated in photographs—beloved visages of friends and family, journeys to far-flung lands, moments crystallized in time. The mattress was bedecked in my favored bedclothes, enfolding me in a semblance of familiarity and comfort. As the first week drew to a close, the erstwhile sterile environs began to transfigure into warmer, more inhabited quarters. Knickknacks blossomed upon the shelves, reading materials amassed atop the coffee table, vestiges of home cooking clustered beside the sink. I had friends, new and old. I watched the sunrise, welcoming my new life, emerging from a cocoon of bright pinks and oranges. Piece by piece, personalized flourish by flourish, my new abode metamorphosed from an unadorned shell into a nest imbued with the unique patina of my life.

Fractals (Samsung Galaxy S8)
Anushka Trivedi, 12
Maryland

Two Poems

By Sierra Elman, 14
California

blue

peace.
inhale, exhale.
i trace shapes in the
mist forming on the
shower wall. a heart.

my heart.
it beats against my ribs.
rhythmically, like
the hot water running in
cascades over my shoulders.

rain.
i listen to it harmonize,
singing against
the windowpanes. i embrace
myself in a towel. lamb's fur.

i count to ten.
exhale, inhale.
peace.

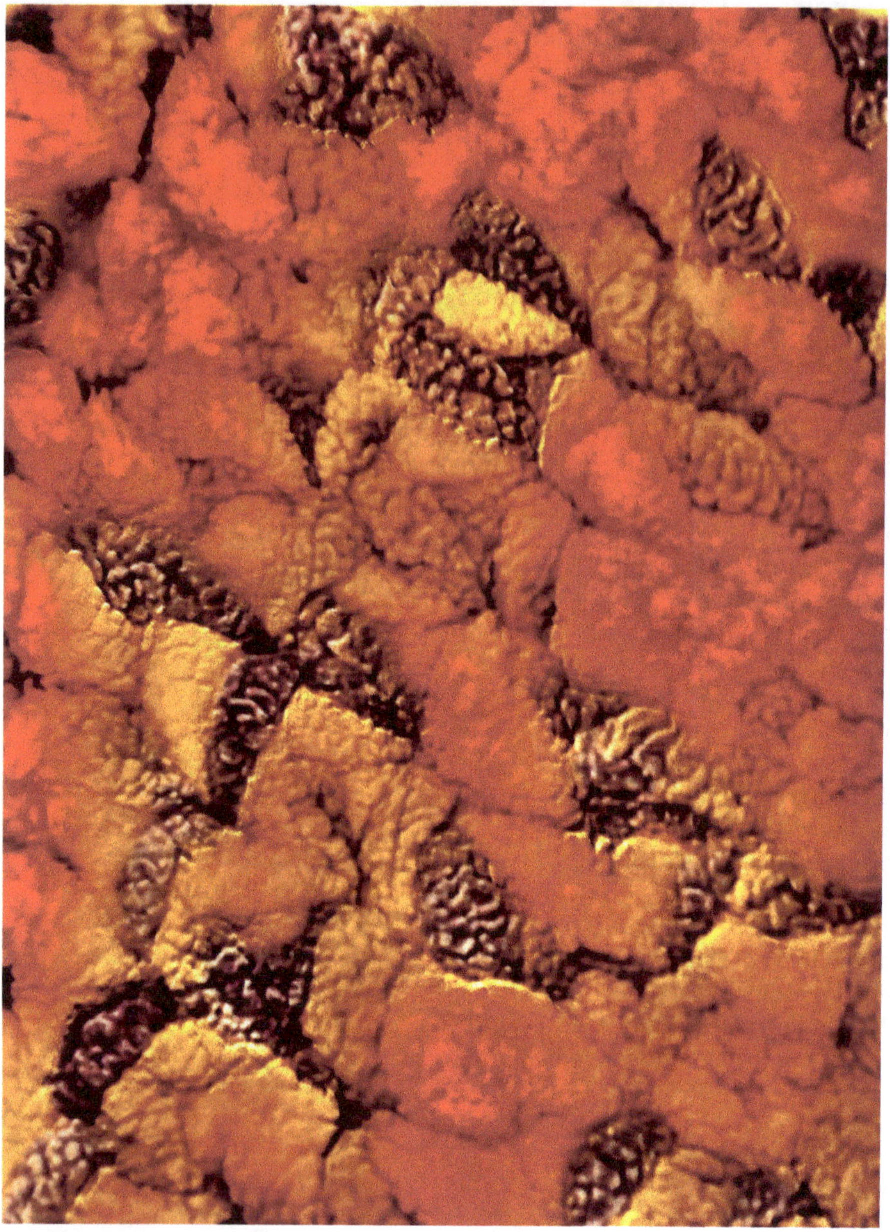

Flaming Blankets (iPhone 15 Pro)
Roi Aeder, 7
New York

yellow

i close my eyes

& tangle my fingers
in threads of sunlight.

i braid strands.
kiss them on their foreheads.
they taste like the lustrous

cream pastries nana used to
bake. i crisscross them over
the ceiling. skinny strings of

gold. i revel in my talent.

when i was little, nana nestled me
in the crook of her leathery arm &
carried me to meet the sun. he

patted my cheek but my skin
did not burn. i was a miracle.

darkness seeps
into my periphery.

my eyes open.

The Flowerpot (Pencil and acrylic paint)
Stuti Jain, 13
Wisconsin

Untitled

By Nadia Darity, 13
Florida

I want to see the stars.
Untainted by city lights.
Unobscured by cloudy nights.
From my porch, they seem as dim as distant flashlights, but I know they are
  so bright.

Take me to a field.
A field with blossoming wildflowers and morning dew on the grass.
I'll bring a blanket if you bring cookies and a jar of milk.
I promise as we look toward the heavens, it will feel like we're laying on
  a bed of silk.

Because there's a fullness that only comes from immersing yourself in creation
  and recognizing the craftsmanship of the creator.
Pause.
Breathe in, and out.
Eight billion people live in the world.

And we all can be guilty of forgetting that it's not mortal trees that give us the air
  we breathe.

A thousand poems tell the tales of love and loss.
And I could write a thousand more, but this one is for ...
The one who breathed into my lungs and hung the stars in my sky.

Fall 1 (Acrylic)
Jason Jun, 14
New Jersey

War and Pieces (Part III)

Misha and his mother flee their war-torn home in Ukraine

By Alice Pak, 13
Ohio

This is the final installment of Alice Pak's novella, which we have been publishing over the course of three issues. If you are a new subscriber, you can read the first two installments online in the March/April and May/June 2024 issues.

Chapter Four

Two weeks slipped by accidentally in a blur of school, TV, and Varya coming over to hang out on the weekends. I barely had time to look around before I found myself standing in the sixth-floor lobby, looking into our half-empty apartment and my mom rolling a suitcase full of clothes out the door. She sighed and turned to me with a pained smile.

"Well," she said, her voice shaky, "time to say goodbye."

"But it's not forever, right?" I asked, readjusting the straps of my backpack.

"No, of course not," she reassured me. "We'll come back one day."

"I already can't wait."

We stood there in silence for another moment, looking at the living room. The worn gray couch. The pale orange curtains fluttering gently to the air conditioning. The drawings, books, and photos standing on the short coffee table. The smell of strawberries and freshly washed clothes.

"Misha? Ho—what's going on?"

I spun around to find Varya, dressed in a rain jacket and boots, staring at me with a lost look on her face. My mom raised an eyebrow at me, frowning.

"You didn't tell her?" she asked.

I looked down at my sneakers.

Varya scanned my face worriedly as the silence became deafening. "Tell me what?"

"We're leaving," my mom said in a flat tone, which indicated both her disappointment towards my behavior and her desire to avoid all negotiations.

"Leaving?" Varya hesitated. "Leaving where?"

"I'm sorry," I mumbled under my breath. "I totally forgot to tell you . . . we have to return to Russia."

Varya didn't reply immediately and instead just stood there, her eyes flickering between me and my mom in disbelief.

"W-what?" she finally managed. "What do you mean? You mean like . . . forever?"

I reached a hand out to her helplessly. "No, no, not forever. Forever is a long time. Just for . . ."

"A few months," my mom picked up for me.

Varya's lip quivered, small rivers of water streaking down her face. She sniffled, rubbing her nose with her sleeve. I felt tears well up in my eyes as well, blurring my vision as my mom shook my shoulder.

"I know it's a lot to take in," she was saying to Varya, her voice seeming to come from miles away as if I was in one of those dreams where you felt like everything was moving through mounds of sand, "but I promise it won't be as bad as it seems. Okay? You'll see each other again before you know it, and I'm sure Misha will have all sorts of new experiences to share with you. This is just a temporary precaution."

Varya sobbed again, nodding shakily. I ran to her and wrapped my arms around her, hugging her tightly. She hugged me back, her fingers digging into my back as if she didn't want to let go. Her warm breath came out in ragged sobs, and I felt a strange sad cloud come over me like a cold shadow, shielding me from any happiness I had been clinging to before.

She finally pulled away after a minute, her eyes still red from crying.

"Promise you'll call me when you can, okay?" she told me, holding my hand in hers. "I will," I said, despite the lump in my throat. I squeezed her fingers.

My mom clicked her tongue, checking her silver watch. "Well, I'm sorry to ruin your goodbyes, but we have to get going, unfortunately. I got us a taxi to drive to the furthest outskirts of the town where the bus station is, and they just texted me that they're waiting for us around the block."

She leaned down and embraced Varya gently, holding her for a second before straightening back up and tucking a stray wisp of hair behind Varya's ear.

"I'll miss you, sweetie," she whispered with a melancholy smile. "I already can't wait to see you again."

"Me too," I chimed in, wiping a tear off my face. "I'll miss you so much."

"Bye," Varya said gloomily, waving after us half-heartedly as the doors of the elevator closed in front of my face.

I can't say anything extremely eventful happened after then. Maybe I was just numb. Maybe I was just tired and forlorn and heartbroken and the entire package. Or maybe there was a small dose of truth in the fact that the entire taxi ride to the train station there was downpouring rain.

The train station didn't make a statement either. In fact, at first I thought that surely our driver was mistaken; he dropped us off at some dump in the middle of nowhere with a couple of empty crates and very few equally empty people, tipped his hat as my mom tipped his change, and drove away as fast as the speed limit on the nearest highway would allow him.

I crinkled my nose at the truck that stood several feet away from us.

Let me make this clear: it wasn't a bus. It wasn't even remotely close to deserving the title of being named a bus. It was a cargo truck at best. A small front cabin where a buff, angry-looking driver sat impatiently chewing a toothpick was roped together with a long black box-looking thing, the door to which was open, and people stood on the ramp, talking hurriedly. On both sides of the truck were bright ads of some cereal company with smiling faces and one too many unconvincing exclamation marks added to make any sense at all.

Turns out, we were about to be smuggled across the border. Semi-illegally.

"We can't just stroll to the other side," my mom explained to me hours later as we sat next to each other, pressed up against the walls of the truck as it rumbled over rocky terrains and we bounced around in the darkness. "Both sides will shoot us without questions. This is by far the safest way to travel and, well, if others have done it, we'll survive too."

"How much longer?" I whined.

My legs ached from being in the same uncomfortable position for the last five hours. My sweater was starting to make my back itch really bad, but if I didn't grip my seat, I'd be thrown against the floor at the next bump. I was starting to get a little carsick, and not being able to see outside a window of sorts made me feel claustrophobic. Was this how Varya felt to be buried under rubble? I waved the thought away instantly, not wanting to think about it.

"I'm sorry, dear." My mom kissed the top of my head. "I'm guessing a few more hours? I believe we're almost halfway there. We passed both the Ukrainian and Russian border controls a few hours ago, and now we just need to get out of the Russian half of the warzone. It's still very dangerous out there right now."

I rested my head against her shoulder, listening to the groan of the tires beneath us slamming into the rough, dirt-packed road. I breathed in the scent of hot, dusty air. Slowly, I found myself being rocked to sleep.

Twisting. Turning. Tumbling down. Flying through the air. Falling.

Screaming. Shouting. Footsteps pounding against the ground. Hands shaking me awake. "Huh?" I mumbled, cracking my eyes open.

"Get up." My mom's frantic voice pierced through my dazed mind, making my brain switch gears as I sat up. "We need to run. Fast."

"Where?" I shouted as she grabbed me by the hand and we stumbled outside.

The truck lay in a ditch on a hill by the side of the road, one of its tires completely deflated. Another one seemed to have popped off completely and

The truck lay in a ditch on a hill by the side of the road, one of its tires completely deflated.

been left behind somewhere on the road. Judging by the small mob of our fellow passengers crowding around the driver, the situation wasn't looking good.

"—so we'll have to walk," he finished as me and my mom joined the group.

"All the way to—?" someone in the back asked.

"Station 415," the driver replied gruffly, looking back at the fallen truck in resentment.

"You're saying we're about to walk eight miles because a tire flew off?" a woman asked, searching something on her phone. "Come on. I'm sure we can fix this."

"*No!*" the driver lunged at her device like a mad cat. "Power your phone off immediately! Don't you know they're tracking us as we speak?"

The lady stared at him, horrified, and slipped the phone in her bag. Another passenger let out a low whistle.

"We better start stridin', folks," he said nonchalantly. "That's a darn long walk. Might take us like half the day with all these kids." He gestured to me and a few toddlers on the hands of their mothers.

I frowned. "I'm not a kid," I protested.

He smirked at me, nodding. "All right. Whatever you say. My point is, let's not waste more time talkin'. Every minute is precious."

Everyone agreed, grumbling. The bus driver took a tattered map out of his back pocket and grudgingly began tracing our further route through the mudland prairie beyond. Some people grabbed any leftover possessions from the truck. My mom fished out a few clean T-shirts and a thick coat from her suitcase before shoving it in the corner of the deserted vehicle with a sigh.

"Aren't you taking it?" I wondered, surprised.

My mom shook her head. "We can't afford it. Walking as far as we're about to is hard enough with the clothes on our backs, let alone any other objects getting in our way."

"Come on, come on! Let's get moving. Chop chop!" a voice hollered.

It had been so long, I'd lost track of time. We'd been walking for many hours. Maybe two. Maybe six. Maybe half a day, for heaven's sake. The scenery changed every couple of miles, from mudland swamps to prairies with tall wild grasses to a lush green forestry. I stared at the road in front of me without looking up. I was so exhausted that I didn't even notice when someone poked my shoulder until I heard a voice in my ear.

"Hey, l'il man. Won't you look up?"

I raised my head and looked at the young man talking to me, confused, until he pointed in the distance. I squinted, and to my great elation, I spotted a small cabin-like structure a few feet away. At the steps of it stood a man dressed in army gear holding a gun, but he didn't point it at us. Instead, he lowered it slowly as our group approached the station, sizing us up.

"Hello, comrade," our driver said, reaching out a tentative hand to the soldier.

The soldier looked at him and his outstretched hand, his gaze calculating yet a smile tugging at the corner of his lips. "Where do you come from?"

"Avdiivka, Ukraine," my mom piped up, "We were traveling to seek refuge when our truck broke down past the border control. We walked here from there."

"Your truck broke down?" The soldier raised an eyebrow. "How so?"

Our driver shrugged, scratching the back of his head. "We don't know. Wheel popped off."

"I see. You're saying you walked eight miles from there?"

"Approximately," my mom inserted again. "With the children it was much slower." The Russian nodded thoughtfully, looking down at me. I held his eyes, unwavering.

"Very well," he said, clapping our driver on the shoulder. "Please, come inside. There you will find food, clothes, and central heating."

Gratefully mumbling thank-yous, our group shuffled in. Inside, we discovered, the station was exactly as small as it seemed: a few small coffee tables in front of a couch leaning against one of the walls, badges and banners hung up on the rest of them. A collection of certificates and maps were cluttered on a desk pushed against the side wall, where there were several computers and landlines running at the same time. A steel door led to another room further in the station, but from the look of it, it was locked pretty heavily. Another soldier stood up as we flooded the room, saluting to his comrade and turning to us with a skeptical look.

"Do you have your passports on you? Did you pass border control? Where was your destination?" He peppered us with questions without pausing for breath.

"We did *not* just walk all this way to be sent back *there*," the young man from our group grumbled, folding his arms across his chest.

"Please," my mom said gently. "We just need to get to somewhere safe."

"Do you have Russian passports?"

Half of our company muttered inaudible responses in agreement. The man's expression softened to what almost looked like a smile.

"All right." He nodded, sitting down behind the desk in the corner and putting on a pair of headphones. "I can arrange for you to be taken to St. Petersburg. This area isn't safer than where you came from, since the Ukrainian military has been shooting back at us."

My mom nodded eagerly. The soldier gave a quick half-smile and turned on his microphone before pelting a string of quiet directions into it, his fingers dancing across the keyboard.

The army truck arrived promptly the next morning at six. I wasn't much too flattered, having to wake up so early after another mostly sleepless night, but, yawning, I let myself get ushered onboard. Rubbing my eyes as someone slipped a box with scrambled eggs and toast into my hands, I found myself sitting somewhere cramped between a leather seat and metal bars. I yelped.

"Chill out, kid," another Russian army man called back, looking me in the eyes through the mirror. "You're not arrested. This was the biggest car the corps had, but unfortunately it's typically used for escorting criminals."

I shook my head, my eyes wide. Oh, the stories I would have to tell.

We drove for maybe two hours, three. I perked up once I started seeing tall, gray buildings spring up around us, flickering past us as we speeded down the highway. The sky was a depressing shade of light gray as well, unlike the blue oceans at the border. Cars honked in every direction. Traffic lights flashed faster than ever, hurting my eyes.

"Are we there yet?" I whispered to my mom, whose eyes seemed to be lighting up with excitement as we drove closer and closer to her hometown.

"We're almost there," she whispered back. "I'm starting to recognize some places... look, to the left is the subway. And if you keep turning right for a couple of blocks, you'll get to the concert hall."

I smiled at my mom's childish enthusiasm, wondering how it would feel to me, coming back to Avdiivka after decades of living someplace else. Would I be happy? Would I be mournful? Would I even want to be there?

The truck dropped us off somewhere in the suburbs of St. Petersburg, and we wobbled out, our legs feeling like jelly. Several pedestrians shot us sharp looks, which I ignored.

"Thank you so much," my mom said to our military driver, shaking his hand.

He saluted us cheerfully. "Proud to serve."

We backed up as the vehicle spun around and left, a trail of smoke curling behind it. I waved behind it, hoping some of the other passengers would wave back, though through the tinted windows, I couldn't see. I'll never know.

My mom exhaled loudly.

"We're here," she announced, unable to contain her excitement.

Dialing a number quickly on her phone, she raised it to her ear, tapping her foot the same way I do when I can't wait for the line to connect. Finally, it did.

"Sergey!" she exclaimed. "Oh, it's so great to hear you again. Me and Misha just got to the city. What?... yeah, naturally. No, it's all good... mhm."

She adjusted the button of my coat.

"Now? You want to pick us up now?" I heard her say. "Well, you don't need to if it isn't a good time... no, I'm sure I could find a hotel of sorts... you're right, I know, it's the middle of the city, but I remember—goodness gracious, you think I don't remember my birthtown?"

I squatted down and inspected a half-ripped leaf floating in a tiny puddle nearby like a boat sailing across a beautiful sea. The moon reflected in the water perfectly, like a mirror, and I wondered if this is what all nights could be like. Calm.

The moon reflected in the water perfectly, like a mirror, and I wondered if this is what all nights could be like. Calm.

" . . . Thank God. You're a lifesaver," my mom finished. "All right, thank you so much . . . yep, see you in a few." She hung up.

"My brother will pick us up in a minute," she practically squealed, and I grinned. "I don't believe you've ever met your uncle, did you, Mishka?"

She ruffled my hair.

"This will be wonderful," she continued dreamily. "He said he has some space in his apartment for the two of us. And your second cousins live a short drive away as well! Oh, you'll love it here, I promise you."

I nodded slightly, still feeling dampened by the intermittent rain and the weight of everything on my shoulders. How could I be thinking of restarting my life here, in one of the greatest cities in the world, while my best friend was all bundled up in her apartment, scared of going out in the street? How could my mom be so happy when people were dying by the thousands, unable to finish living the lives they deserved? How could *anyone* be calm when the world was tearing itself apart, brother waging war against brother?

It has to end, I decided, because we're one nation. One people. One Earth. And if we're going to live together, we should live in agreement and harmony.

We must live in peace.

Epilogue

I walk down the wet sidewalk, kicking a pebble. The rain has stopped, but raindrops fall down on me off of the leaves on the lonely trees lining either side of the pathway like servants in a mansion. Every street is dotted with gray brick buildings with people pouring in and out of doorways, laughing, talking, yelling at their phones. I turn the corner and jog across the road to the small park square on the other side, hearing the slosh of a taxi running over a puddle. There's no people here, only an occasional squirrel scurrying on the benches or an acorn dropping from branches above. It looks a lot like Avdiivka.

I wonder where Varya is now. Of course, I already know the answer. She's in Poland. Her family would get evacuated there when things got really messy. Somewhere in the countryside, maybe in the city. She'll be twelve soon; that's how old I was when I left. When I left her behind.

Maybe she plays violin. She always wanted to learn violin; she used to drag me to concerts and recitals so I could listen with her, and I remember the spark in her amber eyes that would light up every time a bow hit the strings. She used to say that she'd learn my favorite songs on violin so that I'd listen to her play all night and all day. I'd laugh and tease her about never being patient enough to learn such a virtuoso instrument, but she rolled her eyes and shook her head at that every time.

Maybe she has many city friends. Varya made friends easier than I ever did; she just had such a bright, bubbly personality that everyone fell in love with her and her hunger for adventures. I stuck with the same group of classmates I played soccer with every day at recess every year up until I left, but she seemed to gain friends every second. What are friends like in Poland? Did she have to learn Polish? Maybe she goes shopping with them on weekends and they buy ice cream at the mall while they browse through aisles of jeans and dresses. Does she still like strawberry? It was her favorite since forever.

Maybe she forgot about me. I wonder that often, especially on sleepless nights when I get up and stare out the window at the sad streets below and all the hooded strangers walking past. Does she still remember her best friend? Am I still her best friend? It's been so long since I hugged her. Scratch that, it's been so long since I've *talked* to her. Even *written* to her.

I pull out my pocket sketchbook, the one I always drew birds in when I birdwatched by the old swing set in Avdiivka. I fish a pencil stub out of my jacket pocket as well and set the tip down on the paper, thinking.

"Dear Varya,
It's been such a long time since I've last seen you. Almost two years have gone by but still, every day I wake up and remember how you'd bang on my door on Saturdays."

I paused with a smile and added,

"Begging for pancakes."
"How's Poland? I hope you like it there. St. Petersburg is really cool, honestly. There's theaters and concert halls and lots of parks here, and a whole lot more people. Also royal palaces and museums full of things saved from hundreds of years ago. Hundreds of years, you understand? I went to one where there was an entire room made out of real amber. You'd love it here. It's a really big, interesting place compared to Avdiivka.

I go to a Russian school now. I mean, a completely Russian school. It's not much different. We learn the same subjects and still have lunch and recess the same way we used to. My mom signed me up for soccer, so now I play that too outside of school. Maybe one day you can come to one of my matches and root for my team! Games get pretty intense when we play against other districts.

I miss Avdiivka pretty badly. I don't know what shape it was in when you left, but I still remember it as the small, cozy town where we grew up. Wikipedia says it's a ghost town now. Well, that's okay too. We'll come back, I promise. Okay? I know the war tore it down and it seems like there's no hope left. But there's always hope. If no one will rebuild it, we will. We will reconstruct every building, restore every park. We'll take the pieces and glue them together, one by one. It won't be War and Pieces anymore, it will be Peace. No matter how long it takes, we will bring it back."

I lifted my eyes up to the sky, tapping the pencil to my lips, thinking. My emotions were a colorfully stirred up salad that I didn't seem to have the words to pour out on paper. Too much would still be left unsaid, so why not leave it vague?

A soccer ball bumped into my ankle, making me jolt out of my thoughts as I looked around to see who had thrown it.

"Um, excuse me?" a small voice next to me said.

I looked down at a little boy dressed in soccer shorts and a jersey observing me with a guilty smile on his face. He gestured to the ball.

"Oh, is this yours?" I asked, picking it up and tossing it to him. The boy caught it, elated.

"Thank you." He beamed, brushing some wet grass off the sides. "I was just practicing and—"

"You like soccer?" I nodded, smirking. He reminded me of myself when I was younger: carefree, innocent. Besides, he didn't seem to have company with him. How could he possibly play a good game of soccer on his own?

"Yup," he said smartly, pointing at the crest on his chest, "I want to be in the World Cup one day!"

I laughed, standing up and flicking my wrist towards the small field behind the benches. "Want to play a match with me?"

The kid stared at me with a surprised, almost disbelieving expression on his face. "Really? You bet!"

He sprinted away, yelling at me to follow. I smiled to myself, pocketing my notebook and trotting behind him, watching his yellow shirt bounce up and down.

Maybe there *was* still a little light in the world. There was hope after all.

These children will be our future.

Highlight from Stonesoup.com

From the Stone Soup Blog

An Essay on Outrage

By Schamil Saaed, 11
Texas

Have you ever heard your parents say, "Back in my day, life was so much more difficult. Kids these days are so spoiled"? You would be surprised to know that they were the spoiled hipsters of yesteryear.

As long as there have been *Homo sapiens*, there has been a generation gap and elders frowning upon it. One can almost imagine a geriatric Neanderthal rolling his eyes as his progeny used the wheel or even before that, a *Homo erectus* grandfather looking suspiciously at his children living the easy life by using a fire to cook, leaving the good old days of raw meat dinners.

From the complaints of Socrates turning young men against the establishment to the small but vocal groups of Boomers on social media, there have been many examples of elderly backlash to changing times. One of the first documented episodes of such outrage goes back to Ancient Greece, from the fifth century BCE onwards. During this time, a population boom and plentiful sustenance inspired philosophers and thinkers to question the world around them. In fact there is a saying, "All that I know is that I know nothing." The young Athenians were educated to question everything, and this stung the established order. The noblemen condemned this wave of change and even succeeded in poisoning the leader of a major group, whom we know as Socrates, in 399 BCE. But the die was cast, and his doctrine spread under the likes of Aristotle and Alexander the Great. Despite the cry of the previous generations, change was inevitable.

During the Industrial Revolution, from around 1800-1915, technology started ramping up, and new discoveries began to replace the established order. The younger generation of this period shook the world with the printing press and steam engines, as well as telegraphs. Gone were the days of horse-drawn carriages, messenger pigeons, and quill pens. As an example of such geriatric backlash, the famous Luddites smashed machines in textile plants all across southern England, but the resistance was quelled by 1815, and the rest was history.

You can read the rest of Schamil's piece at https://stonesoup.com/post/an-essay-on-outrage-by-schamil-saaed-11/.

About the Stone Soup Blog

We publish original work—writing, art, book reviews, multimedia projects, and more—by young people on the Stone Soup Blog. You can read more posts by young bloggers, and find out more about submitting a blog post, here: https://stonesoup.com/stone-soup-blog/.

Honor Roll

Welcome to the Stone Soup Honor Roll. Every month, we receive submissions from hundreds of kids from around the world. Unfortunately, we don't have space to publish all the great work we receive. We want to commend some of these talented writers and artists and encourage them to keep creating.

FICTION

Logan Francis, 12
Mia Goldschmidt, 10
Gary Gong, 9
Eden Kendall, 10
Aria Po, 9

MEMOIR

Emma Brandt, 12
Lucas Castro, 9
Joshua Choi, 13
Annabel Feng, 11
Noa Gartrell, 11
Alexander Milone, 11
Rafael Moura, 11
Ezra Park, 11
Zoe Rossides, 12
Jackson Steinberg, 11
Ava Szekretar, 11

POETRY

Nandika Agrawal, 10
Teresa Cheng, 11
Owen Miller Noel, 10
Unni Odman, 10
Ellie Wang, 11

ART

John Wang, 9

Visit the Stone Soup Store at Amazon.com/stonesoup

At our store, you will find . . .

- Current and back issues of *Stone Soup*
- Our growing collection of books by young authors, as well as themed anthologies
- Journals and sketchbooks

. . . and more!

Finally, don't forget to visit Stonesoup.com to browse our bonus materials. There you will find:

- Information about our writing workshops
- Monthly flash contests and weekly creativity prompts
- Blog posts from our young bloggers on everything from sports to sewing
- Video interviews with *Stone Soup* authors

. . . and more content by young creators!

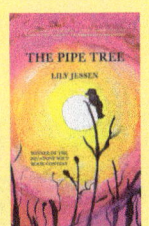

Scan this to visit *Stone Soup* online!

Printed in the USA
CPSIA information can be obtained
at www.ICGtesting.com
CBHW070255090624
9690CB00001B/1